T0131629

ALSO BY ELIZABETH HESS STAMPER

BELIEVING IN LOVE:
Sexuality and Healing
in Spiritual Relationship

The Butterfly Book

The Inner Journey to the Beloved

E LIZABETH H ESS S TAMPER

BALBOA.
PRESS
A DIVISION OF HAY HOUSE

Front cover image credit: Derek Gores
Author photo credit: Daniel Kasser

Balboa Press books may be ordered through booksellers or by contacting:

Balboa Press
A Division of Hay House
1663 Liberty Drive
Bloomington, IN 47403
www.balboapress.com
1 (877) 407-4847

Because of the dynamic nature of the Internet, any web addresses or links contained in this book may have changed since publication and may no longer be valid. The views expressed in this work are solely those of the author and do not necessarily reflect the views of the publisher, and the publisher hereby disclaims any responsibility for them.

The author of this book does not dispense medical advice or prescribe the use of any technique as a form of treatment for physical, emotional, or medical problems without the advice of a physician, either directly or indirectly. The intent of the author is only to offer information of a general nature to help you in your quest for emotional and spiritual well-being. In the event you use any of the information in this book for yourself, which is your constitutional right, the author and the publisher assume no responsibility for your actions.

Any people depicted in stock imagery provided by Thinkstock are models, and such images are being used for illustrative purposes only. Certain stock imagery © Thinkstock.

Print information available on the last page.

ISBN: 978-1-5043-4219-3 (sc)
ISBN: 978-1-5043-4220-9 (e)

Library of Congress Control Number: 2015916331

Balboa Press rev. date: 1/21/2016

For Mike

Beloved,

I have searched

The Universe for you,

Until at last I knew—

I must find you first

Within my heart.

When I have found you there,

Then I will find you

Everywhere.

Contents

Acknowledgements

Thank you to my beautiful family and friends for the encouragement, support and wisdom you so generously share with me. Your gifts of kindness and insight made it possible for me to believe in this love, live this story and write this book.

In particular, thank you to Nellie Brannan for the gift of the journal, the Butterfly Book. Also, heartfelt thanks to Daylight Kumpa, Kristie Ferriell, Renelle West, Ingrid Helander, Margie Ruzzo, Ted Riskin, Amanda Vargas and Patricia Mulreany—in so many ways you have each held sacred space around the cocoon, allowing for transformation and creation, and I am deeply grateful.

Thank you to my two sisters, Bhekaji Lynch and Lucinda Kasser, for loving and believing in me, and for nourishing me, body, mind and soul.

To my children and grandchildren, wow! You are each amazing in so many ways and you fill my life with *immeasurable* joy.

And to my husband, Mike, thank you for saying *yes* and living *yes* and for everything that follows from that simple, sensual, spiritual, and life-changing word.

The Inspiration

What follows is a love story that also happens to be true. Every day for over a month, I was inspired to write letters to someone that I had never met. In fact, when I started, I wasn't even sure that he existed. This someone was my "unknown Beloved" and I wrote to him because I wanted to believe in him, to forge a connection with him, and ultimately, to attract the flesh-and-bones realness of him into my life. All of this happened. He became real to me and I fell in love with him. And then, one day, he showed up. Many years later, we are still and so gratefully together. Although our "happily ever after" has not always been easy (this is, after all, a true story and not a fairy tale), our life together keeps getting better, sweeter, and richer in every way. And our love for each other is in depth and breadth and beauty truly beyond what I could have imagined.

For years writing has been a part of my spiritual practice. Putting pen to paper has helped me sort through thoughts and feelings, find relief and release, and consciously change my moods, beliefs and attitudes. I have journaled almost daily to connect to Spirit, to record and relive precious moments, and, importantly, to *practice* being kind and affirming to myself. Through writing I've discovered insights and aspects in me that I may not have found any other way.

Writing the letters to this hoped-for stranger did all of the above for me—and more, much more. On my balcony that overlooked a small lagoon, I would start the day with meditation. Then, cat at my feet and coffee in hand, I would take up my pen and pour out my heart. I soon discovered, however, that there was something different about this writing: I was writing to *him,* and it was intimate and personal. It was a sensual experience as well—holding the open book in my lap, grasping the pen, my hand moving across the pages and watching blue ink flow out onto smooth paper. It has been said that writing a letter to someone in this way is a *caress.*[1] Indeed, every morning I was sending energetic caresses to my Beloved.

The relationship became real to me very quickly. I was spending time with him and enjoying it immensely. Some might wonder if I were using fantasy to escape a lonely reality. Perhaps. Fantasy is defined as an act of the imagination, and the dictionary warns us that it is "far removed from normal reality". And yet everything ever created or accomplished in "normal reality" began as a dream or an idea, as *just a fantasy* in someone's mind. But what if, in fact, fantasy opens us to another dimension of reality, one in which truly everything is possible? In the awareness state opened to me through writing the letters, the usual notions of time and space did not limit my loving connection with another. Nor did the lack of any known history with each other. And in this dimension, I discovered a love that transcends duality and teaches the truth of Oneness. In this place, I first met my Beloved.

~~~~

If there is a reality that we want to know, using the God-given faculty of our imagination can be the first part of the journey there. And if our heart longs for a sacred, intimate relationship, writing can help us focus our imagination and shift our own energy from doubt to faith and from fear to love. As we become more trusting and more loving, we will naturally attract those who mirror these qualities. And, if imagination and a dedicated spiritual practice can transform us and summon the Beloved, could it not also usher in a happier, healthier, and more peaceful world?

Throughout history, we honor and admire those who were able to envision and accomplish things that seemed impossible to most people of their time. They also worked hard and inspired others to believe in the dream too. But we don't call them *efforters*, we call them *visionaries*. All the great visionaries imagined a better world—not just for themselves, their families or a certain class or group of people—but for everyone. The more inclusive a vision is, the more powerful it is, and the bigger the dream we can hold and tend, the more energy we will summon into and through us. While I was writing the letters, it became more and more clear to me that I wanted this relationship to serve not just me but others as well. Given our interdependence with everyone and everything, how could it not? Seeing my desire for a relationship in this light also allowed me to feel more surrendered and more at peace with how or when—or even if—it would happen at all.

~~~~

Albert Einstein wrote that imagination was more important than knowledge because "knowledge is limited to all we now know and understand, while imagination embraces the entire world, and all there ever will be to know and understand." May our collective imagination create a vision of a world that we truly want—so that we will be inspired to nurture, love and work for it . . . a Beloved World for ourselves, for our children and for all future generations.

The beginning of this book, Part One, tells how I came to write the letters to my unknown Beloved. In Part Two are the letters themselves. In Part Three, I describe how we met and fell in love with each other in "real time".

The journal in which I wrote was a reprint of a Japanese book called *A Flight of Butterflies*[2] that was originally published in 1904. In Japan, books are read from (what would be to us) back to front. So, on a whim, I penned my first letter in the back of the book and wrote my way toward the front. With each day and with each letter, it felt as if I were moving closer to a *beginning*. However, in the book you are holding, the letters are printed in what would be the "right" order to the Western mind. Ah, the persistent dualities of this world—back/front, right/wrong, east/west, stranger/lover! And yet, contrast can serve to steer us toward what we want, and without it how colorless life would be. May this story encourage us to allow and yet move beyond the dualities to the place where the Beloved is met, and is both *other* and *none other* than our deepest Self.

In a few short words, here then is the message of this book: Dream it, write it, and enjoy your vision fully—until one day you wake up and see that you are living it. And you are not alone in the new reality.

But then, you never really were.

Part One

The Vision

Your longing desires to take you towards the absolute realization of all the possibilities that sleep in the clay of your heart; it knows your eternal potential, it will not rest until it is awakened.

~ *John O'Donohue*

Friends, let those whose Beloved
is absent write letters—
~ Mirabai

The Path to Your Heart

I magine that someone you love is coming to visit. In
fact, you enjoy this person so much that you're hoping
that she will stay a while. So, the first thing you do is look
around your home and see what needs to change to make
your space more beautiful and your guest as comfortable
as possible. You find yourself attuning to your guest and
feeling into what might make her happy. So you clean
and clear and rearrange—and consciously fill your home
with the energy of love.

This book is about inspiring you to prepare your inner
space, your mind and heart, so that the Beloved will come
and want to stay. Who is "the" Beloved? In one sense,
in that precious moment when love and appreciation
are flowing through you toward another—*that one* is
the Beloved. Humans have the potential to know and
love everyone in this whole-hearted way, and the more
we heal and grow and awaken, we will experience this
immediate and unconditional love more and more often
and with more and more people. But in this book, the
word "Beloved" refers to the person with whom you

share or want to share a sacred, intimate, and committed relationship. This is the Soul Friend that you want to be with, make love to, and adore for the rest of your days. This is the one who wins your heart—even as they break it wide open for Life to enter more deeply.

> *So, how do lovers find each other? Within this vast universe that holds us all, what is the homing device of the heart? How do I find you, Beloved, amongst the billions of humans on this small, perfect planet amidst the billions of galaxies in the Universe?*

Actually, there is a way in which *how* is the wrong question here. *How, when, where* tend to land us in our left-brains. These questions are better for filling in details and logistics than for birthing new possibilities. When we want to create something new in our life, it helps to investigate *why* we want it. When we ponder *why do I want you, why do I need you, why do I love you*—and then allow and feel the answers arise from within, then the very vibration of the answer begins to summon the Beloved into our life.

Sometimes, however, asking *why* is not, as the Buddhists would say, skillful means. When we look at the past and wonder why something bad has happened, we could be using this as a way to stay in our heads and forestall feeling our pain. And we are only postponing the forgiveness and acceptance that bring peace. When we let go and peace flows in, then often the understanding that we've been seeking comes, too. Asking *why* about the past can become an obsession that delays our healing. But asking *why* about the future can bring clarity to our vision and momentum to our desire.

The love that you want to give calls to the one who wants to receive that very expression of love, that particular fragrance of love. The love that you long to share beckons the one who wants to receive it as surely as the scent of a flower summons the bee and the butterfly. But when your longing is tinged with fear or resistance, then there's still a thicket around you that doesn't let the Beloved come near. Unlike the fairy tales, there is no one strong or charming enough to break through your own defenses to loving and being loved. Getting rid of the thicket is totally up to you. And so, commitment to one's own healing, well-being and growth comes first on the path of relationship. To find the Beloved, we cultivate being the Beloved inside ourselves—which means choosing love over fear every hour of every day. It means finding and loving back into wholeness every lost or wounded part of ourselves. It means learning the skills of being with ourselves in patient, compassionate ways and at the same time strengthening the heart-centered will to keep growing and expanding beyond the circle of our personal concerns. When the felt-answer to *'why do I want you'* is answered with a joyful willingness to serve the greater good and a happy desire to share a beautiful life, then the path to your heart is open and clear.

~~~~

After the end of a long and good marriage and after several years of dating and exploring other relationships, I wanted to find someone with whom there was a future. Or, better said, someone whose idea of the future was similar to mine. I had dated men who wanted more of a future with me than I did and other men whose view of their future didn't include me at all. Lots of fun, heartbreak and learning. And, finally, enough drama! One day I was just done. I was ready to ask those "why questions" in a serious, intentional way:

Why do I want you? I want you, whoever you are, because I want to learn to love more fully and deeply, not holding back for any reason. I want the sweet joy of loving and expressing my love freely.

Why do I need you? I want to know that I am whole and complete as I am but that I can *choose* to need you and to be okay with you needing me. This awareness of needing another is a truer understanding of our interdependence—and a more honest foundation for the vulnerability that allows for real intimacy. I also know that some of my inner obstacles to love will *only* show up when in relationship, and so I need you to mirror for me what those blocks are. Without you, parts of me will stay wounded and buried as there will be no motivation strong enough to go through the discomfort of digging that deeply.

Why do I love you? I love you because it feels good to love you. I love you because of what you bring into my life: companionship, fun, adventure, lovemaking, growth, healing, mutual inspiration, a sacred witness . . . and all the many other blessings yet to be discovered.

All my experiences in relationship finally brought me to the clarity, the decision to wait, in a sense, for the 'real deal'. Not long after that, the letter-writing began and soon I could see that the process was helping me cultivate a new consciousness about relationships. As I wrote to him, I saw more clearly what needed to change *in me*. As old doubts and fears surfaced and released, more peace, equanimity and trust flowed in. As the pages were filling up with loving words, my life was filling up with more and more love. One day, finally, the guest room—the welcoming space in my world—was ready and he arrived. For quite simply, love attracts love. (We always make it way more complicated than that, don't we?) And yet, it always has and it always will.

Failing to fetch me at first, keep encouraged
Missing me one place search another
I stop somewhere waiting for you
~ Walt Whitman

The First Sign

July 4ᵗʰ, Sedona, Arizona

It is 113 degrees, not a breath of wind, and the heat presses down as I walk alone through the canyon. But it is not the only burden I carry today. I broke up with my lover a few months before—for the third (or was it the fourth?) and hopefully the last time. I had spent months battling the urge to run over to his house and say, "Okay, you win! It's all on your terms. I give in just to be with you." I'm past that stage now, but today is one of those days when the feelings—grief, despair, loneliness—are a heavy ache in my chest. *How can emptiness feel so heavy?* I wonder. Maybe I'm not meant to be in relationship. Maybe I want too much. Maybe I can't be nearly selfless or loving or whatever enough to make it last. Maybe it's just better to keep my heart closed to romance and pursue a safe, celibate, more "spiritual" life.

I stop and take a drink from my water bottle and, glancing up, I notice the heat-intensified colors of the Sedona desert: the startling red of steep canyon walls and the towering white clouds against a deep blue sky. Hmmm, red, white and blue—how appropriate for the Fourth of July! The beauty that I see comforts me and I walk on.

The path takes me to the bottom of the canyon and across a dry creek bed. I am trudging through a forest of parched-looking trees and shrubs when the largest butterfly I have ever seen comes fluttering down the path toward me. I stop and watch in amazement as she flies right up to my heart and then away again—back up the path and then off into the woods. I follow her—*have to*—and haven't gone far when I come into a clearing with a large flat stone in the center. The butterfly has disappeared. The altar-like stone is summoning so I take off my backpack and sit on its cool, smooth surface. After a second, I lie down and look up through the trees. Immediately a strong wind starts to blow, making a big noise as the treetops sway and the leaves shudder. For a brief and timeless moment, I am in the center of a swirling, dancing vortex, and then the wind stops—as abruptly as it had begun—and all is still again.

In awe, I stand up and look around me. The oppressive heat has lifted and the very air feels different . . . clean and clear . . . almost sparkling. And then, I realize that my inner burden has lifted as well. I feel light, open, miraculously free.

"Independence Day, yes!"

I smile in wonder, bow in gratitude, and go back to the path.

~~~~

A few days later, I'm at the airport in Phoenix, wandering around while awaiting my flight back home. All of a sudden, I see the butterfly! She's in a glass exhibit case, and I discover that she is a triple swallowtail, the largest butterfly in North America, and her wingspan is as large as my open hand. A short time later, I'm settling into my seat on the plane. I open up the magazine that I'd picked up in Sedona and start reading an article on Native American spirituality. "They understood that Spirit speaks to them through all of the natural world— the plants and animals, and especially through the wind. And a big wind carries a big message." I gaze out the small window at the quickly receding Earth and, remembering how the grief and despair were airlifted from my heart, I receive once again the simple message:

A chapter of my life is finally over. A new one can now begin.

*The ancient Greek word for psyche means "butterfly," a
creature who undergoes a long period of metamorphosis in the
chrysalis state before transformation or awakening is possible.*
~ Author Unknown

The Writing Begins

It's another hot day, about a month after my first trip to Sedona, and I'm helping my friend pack up her house to move. She comes across a large, cloth-covered book by a Japanese artist. The book was originally printed in Japan in 1904 and then reproduced by the Metropolitan Museum of Art, and contains the woodblock prints of butterflies. It opens with a short story about a dream, and then a thousand colorful butterflies (and no words) are scattered over the remaining pages. She looks at the book for a long moment, then invites me to sit down with her among the boxes so that she can tell me two stories about the butterfly book.

The first story is about a friend of hers who was in love with a man, a coworker who was married to someone else at the time. Being respectful of his marriage, she kept her feelings to herself. Nevertheless, she loved him deeply and wrote to him every day. She never gave him the letters; she simply put them in a drawer. Two years passed, his marriage ended, and he began to fall in love with the letter-writer. Eventually, he proposed, she accepted, and on their wedding night, she opened that drawer and gave him all the letters.

The second story is about my friend's son. She had given her son a copy of this same book, and in turn, he gave it to his sweetheart with a proposal of marriage written among the butterflies. She said yes.

"Now it's your turn," my friend says, and she hands me the book.

~~~~

The very next morning, after meditation, I sat on my balcony, opened the butterfly book and began to write. *Beloved* . . . Hmm, well, this felt odd. Do I pretend like I know him? Does he exist just in my imagination or is there a real person out there? Feeling a little self-conscious, I wrote the first letter. Gradually, I began to believe in him and the relationship became more and more real. My impatience and frustration were slowly being edged out by inner peace and a kind of contented expectation. For many years, I had worked with the lesson from *A Course in Miracles*[3] that reads, "Only infinite patience produces immediate results", so I knew that, ironically, the less I needed him to show up, the closer to me he actually was. Soon there was a very strong sense of meeting with him almost in a different dimension—not in the future or the past—but in a present that was also outside of time. To be in this present, I needed to be quiet, empty, open. And to feel through my heart. The Beloved became an object of meditation in the best sense of the word—where subject, object and verb are one, and awareness is filled with a spacious and edgeless radiance.

Whenever I would really 'click in' and feel myself align with the energy of this relationship, I would be flooded with a profound sense of him—as if he were just in the next room and at any moment he'd walk through the door. Butterflies or symbols of butterflies would often show up at these times. When these synchronicities would happen, I took it as a sign of that mysterious force, that immutable law of attraction that has been bringing lovers together for a very long time. I began to trust it.

For the next five weeks, I wrote almost every morning, and over time, the content of the letters changed. They became less about something happening on the outer, physical level and more about the inner connection and how it was transforming me. One day, I felt complete with the writing process. My heart was full and my trust in the reality of our relationship had become so strong that I knew that whether I met him tomorrow or in three lifetimes, the timing would be perfect. And so it was. A few days after writing my last letter, I met the man who didn't know that he already had a home within my heart.

~~~~

It is two years after that first trip to Sedona and the encounter with the butterfly, and I am there once again—this time with Michael, my fiancé. We are visiting Stacey, an old friend of his, and she asks me if I'd ever been there before.

"Yes, I was here once before . . . about two years ago."

"Oh, that's funny. The last time Mike was here was about two years ago as well."

"Oh yeah, that's right," he says, "It was the Fourth of July. It was incredibly hot and I remember hiking that long, dry canyon."

"Boynton Canyon," says Stacey.

My eyes get big and I look at Mike. "Umm . . . really? I was there that same day—and I hiked that very same canyon!"

With no small feeling of amazement, we gaze at each other . . . and breathe it in.

Part Two

The Letters

"You would not have called to me
unless I had been calling to you," said the Lion.
~ C.S. Lewis, The Silver Chair

Beloved,

I am at peace this morning. I close my eyes, extend my awareness to you and I can almost feel you. I can almost feel you loving me. The breeze on my face is soft and real—and I'm taking it in as if it were the caress of your affection coming to me.

Oh, this feels good! As I receive this caress, a little bubble of joy arises within me. And as I focus on that joy and breathe into it—it grows . . .

Could it be this simple? I extend my awareness again to you, and I sense waves now, waves of joy. I imagine that right now they are flowing out to you—wherever you are—and at this same moment you are receiving them. Can you feel it? Can you feel this softness upon your face, the breeze of my affection?

Ahh, to send you joy
and to imagine you receiving it
seems like a very good way to begin
loving you.

Beloved,

I do realize that in writing to you, I am really writing to myself. But I also know that in some unexplainable way, you are a part of me, and I want to trust and believe in our oneness . . . more and more and more.

Thank you in advance for recognizing me. And for liking me. (Yeah, let's start there!) Thank you in advance for the joy and the passion—passion for life, for God, and for each other. And thank you, too, for the quiet times and the beauty of just being together.

I come toward you knowing that, much of the time, I do know how to be happy. I've spent years collecting tools and practices for finding joy, for being peaceful—which sometimes I've used out of desperation, sometimes from inspiration, and often from a longing for peace. I trust these practices. I feel grateful for them because it is my happiness that will bring you to me. And it is your happiness that will help me to recognize you.

Beloved,

*I was meditating this morning and feeling so much peace inside—
and suddenly, I was flooded with awareness of all that I have.
And, as always, in that place of utter peace and gratitude and
fullness, I had no desires or needs or longings.*

*But then I came out of meditation and found myself still wanting
you. I don't know how to live in that deep, desireless peace . . .
but I'm okay with that. I see my dream and desire for you as a
gift, and I'm holding this gift inside in a safe place where it can
grow. A dream needs a protected place where it can grow strong—
strong enough to risk the winds of the world. May this journal of
letters be that place. May it be a safe harbor for my dream of you.*

My Dear,

I have not written for several days but have thought of you often. Thinking of you comforts me—like a cool hand on a fevered brow, like a balm of kind words to a worried soul. When I think of you, the very air around me becomes my friend.

The last few days I have been so happy—I have felt this sweet, open and unblemished certainty of the love within all things. And I've found myself breathing this love in—deliberately and gratefully—from everywhere and everything. From the trees, the sun, from the bed I sleep in, the food I eat, the people I meet. Because I believe that everything and everyone is made of this energy of love, I can imagine people loving me even though they may not consciously know or feel it. But because I believe in it, I receive it and feel happy . . . and grateful.

Beloved,

Today I bless you. I bless your mother for birthing you and raising you, and teaching you about gentleness and caring. Today I praise your father for his pride and delight in you. I thank you for being a man strong and kind and good.

Today I acknowledge all the women who have been your lovers, your teachers, and your companions in work and worry and wonderment.

Today I thank the Creator for the design and the brilliant engineering of your soul.

Sometimes I think—with all this gratitude and love and blessing going on—how could you not come to me? When here I am, absorbed in the enjoyment of loving you, happy in the fantasy of you—how could you not come?

Meanwhile, today, right now . . . lean toward me with your heart. Yearn for me and catch my blissful desire for you on the next breeze. Then, come to me. When you're ready, Beloved, come and find me.

Beloved,

Since I've been writing you, I have fallen more in love with my life, with the patterns of my days, the comfort of my nights. And I feel an eagerness too—as if I am so close to stepping into a whole new world. I imagine this world as one that I've been traveling toward my whole life—it's one where no one is a stranger and nothing hides the sacred beauty of creation.

I remember glimpsing the world like this once when I was a child. One day I was gazing at the trees in our backyard and seeing how the sunlight danced on bright green leaves against an intensely blue sky.Although I didn't have words for the experience then, it felt as if in that moment I woke up to the 'Truth' of the world. Through the absolute grace of trees and sky and light and color, there was an opening and a longing. The opening was to really see creation, and to see it as an immeasurable act of love. The longing was to stay in the beauty and to be able to return this love.

Someday, when we find each other in this new world—this world made new by each other—may I share the beauty that I see with you . . . and the beauty that I see in you, too.

Beloved,

My mood is strange today. I feel the familiar longing but with less resistance. It is just another shade, another texture that the atmosphere can wear.

The edge of wanting is sharp, almost painful—but it's not. No, it's not painful because I believe that the edge proves the existence of what is wanted. One of my teachers used to say 'don't resist your longing'. Be grateful for it. Be grateful that you can be like one of Rumi's love dogs who are always crying for the Beloved.

And yet—if you merely distract me from Spirit, then don't come. If I keep you from the truth, then don't come. If (and when) my ego tries to mold you into what it needs or wants from you, then back away fast! But if we can help each other move into the highest spheres of loving that are possible here, then come, my love. Come as quickly as you can.

Sweet Friend,

Oh my, in this yoga of relationship, I have so much to learn and unlearn and practice. I see how old beliefs, habits of thought, have kept me afraid to really let go in love. Instead, I protect. I hide behind the part of me that is strong, capable and independent. God forbid that capable-me should need anything from anyone! But I do. I need to let down the shield and learn that it's not a weakness to need others. I want be able to come up to that moment of choice between fear and love, and let love triumph, over and over, and more and more.

What a strange life this is. Caught in old emotional habits, like a fox in a trap, would I even trust the one who comes to free me from the trap? But, at the same time, I have faith in the possibility of freedom, and my faith in love grows every time I heal another piece of my small story.

So, I keep bringing light in, and try to love the confused one in all her confusion, the protective one in all her fear, the strong one in her weakness, the little one in her neediness. If I can learn to love all the parts of me myself, then I won't burden you so much with that job. You can thank me later for that!

Dearest,

I am thinking now of true friendship—one in which we see each other's essence, and feel seen in that same deep way. Where you look into me and know me through and beyond the layers of history, personality and physicality. Where I look into you, and recognize the Self in you, and know how to remember the love that's there . . . and rest within it.

Is there a difference between my love for God and my love for you? No. I think it is the same. Love for love's sake. Within this huge and holy net of Being, all paths lead back to the heart, and all people are being drawn to the expression of love that will both stretch them and delight them. We too are pilgrims and our paths are leading us, step by step, day by day, to each other.

Of this, I have no doubt.

Just after 9/11

Dearest One,

The heart of the world was once again broken these last few days as we witnessed the horror that humanity is capable of . . . and in this time, I wanted you even more. I wanted to be held in strong, safe arms, and reassured of the Good. The reality and unbrokenness of the Good.

Thank God for friends, for family and spiritual community, for all the places where we can and do give each other comfort, hope, support. I pray that wherever you are, you have that, too. It's strange but my love for everyone and everything seems bigger since this happened. Also, the desire to serve is so alive—I'm seeing it in everyone. And the questioning—how can we bring hope and healing, how can there be peace—these are the conversations around me now.

At the same time, I am even more aware of the inner critical voice—and the judgments, the subtle, most insidious ones, are like nails on the blackboard in my head. Yes, when we are scared, that voice can get loud! It tries to find relief through having someone to blame, but such relief is so short-lived and so dangerous. Because blame calls for punishment . . . and the cycle of violence goes on.

Although I may never get rid of this voice, I pray that I recognize it clearly and see the fear that triggers it. I don't want to not-feel the fear—or any other signal from my instincts or emotions. But I do want to grow my capacity to respond from compassion and understanding . . . and from the real strength of peace.

I pray that you and your loved ones are safe. I pray for peace.

Beloved,

Some days the world doesn't make sense. I glimpse the absurdity of so much—too much—of the crazy, painful stuff that goes on here. Some days I witness more than I can or want to handle. These are the days when I just want to lie down beside you and breathe my way past all thoughts . . . just breathe . . . until we drop off together into stillness, into a deep, soft sleep. It comforts me to imagine that.

So, today was an intense day, and I was really glad to have a way to be helpful. When I'm not focused on helping someone else, it's too easy to get caught up in my own fear. So, is there really such a thing as "selfless service" when I benefit so much from serving? Maybe there is—but maybe only when the small-self stops trying to direct the show and lets go of 'being' the helper.

Meanwhile. May your world make sense today, and if it doesn't, may the craziness you see outside inspire you to seek and find peace inside.
And then, please help to bring it to the world!

Beloved,

I feel so lucky in this moment to know how powerful love is and how much I need it. And to know that—at least some of the time—I know how to love.

The horror of these last few days, the tragedy of 9/11, has brought on a quickening of spirit in those around me. I hear the outpouring of raw emotion from others, and people are not speaking in ordinary language right now. They are speaking in prayer. And the prayer is both the hope and the affirmation that love is the answer, the healing force, the only worthwhile medium of exchange right now. I am seeing such goodness in people, such simple, beautiful goodness in people as they show up to be present for each other, to help, and to offer compassion.

And you, my dear, where are you? What's going through your mind and heart? Perhaps you are also holding ever closer to the ones you love and feeling more gratitude for the simple fact of Life. Perhaps, in the intensity of this time, you are wanting even more—as I am—to find your Beloved.

Dearest,

I'm holding this beautiful book in my lap, this journal in which I am writing to you, and I'm struck by the fact that it's backwards. You see, the original was made in Japan where traditionally books are read from right to left . . . the opposite of how we read here in the West. So I started my letters to you in the back of the book, and day by day I've been working my way toward the front. Somehow, this is also a statement about time.

In my journey towards you, I am collapsing the illusion of linear time and moving backward through these pages to undo my past and create a new future. I am writing my way into a reality that is always present, and into the "experience of eternity right here and now." In this reality, we have known each other always, and yet—we have also just met, for we are at the beginning of a new story. We are the One that has become Two and we are the Two who extend to each other in Oneness. In becoming two, we get to have a mirror and an opposite. We get to know oneness and difference, and the possibility of cocreation. In the Eternal Moment, we join the archetypal dance of Shiva and Shakti, Krishna and Radha, Jesus and Mary Magdalene, light and dark, emptiness and form.

I move backwards to undo the beliefs in illusion, in limitation, in lack that might hold me away from you in time. I move forward to the Beginning of our shared journey in this life. Everywhere I look, I see souls uniting and reuniting for the great adventure of love, and every happy couple reminds that this is what lies ahead for you and me.

Eternity isn't some later time. Eternity isn't a long time.
Eternity has nothing to do with time. Eternity is that dimension
of here and now that thinking and time cuts out.
This is it. If you don't get it here you won't get
it anywhere, and the experience of eternity
right here and now is the function of life.
~ Joseph Campbell

Beloved,

The other day I was at a prayer vigil and I was silently repeating the Healer's Prayer from A Course in Miracles, which begins, "I am here only to be truly helpful." I realized it was a vow, a promise—not unlike the vows we make at a wedding or an ordination. I saw myself standing at an altar, holding a hand and saying the prayer. But in my imagination the one to whom I was promising myself was the soul of the world . . . and I was holding the hand of humanity. May it be so!

But what promises do I want to hear from you? Promise to be patient with me, as best you can. Listen to me when I need to talk and shut me up when I need to listen. Hold me when I need to be held and kiss me whether I need it or not. Laugh with me often so that joy is a song always playing in the house of our Life.

Promise to love God and yourself deeply, passionately, and to never tire of exploring God, yourself and me. I promise all this to you . . . and more.

My heart is more and more ready for you every day.

Sweet Friend,

There is something very powerful that happens when I write to you. I never know if it will happen every time but it's about having this on-going conversation with someone that I believe does exist and does love me. There's something about this love that is almost overwhelming.

Overwhelming: overpowering . . . so great as to render resistance or opposition useless. Feeling this love takes me to a place where I have no fear, no doubt, and, gratefully, no self-consciousness. I'm not even worried that I might say or do something wrong and then be rejected by you. There have been many times in my life where I moved briefly into that space with someone . . . where I felt the certainty of being loved for all of who I am. But it never lasted for more than a few hours, a few days. Even then, I think there was doubt. If he really knew me . . .

So, yes, sometimes the love is overpowering and why on earth would I resist it? Other times, this love brings a sense of joyful calm over me. The energy of our connection to each other is getting stronger. I can step into it and like a warm shower my whole body relaxes. I let go of everything and breathe you in all the way to my toes.

So, thank you for loving me and for the shelter of this relationship, this place where I can be my self. Thank you for the peace of trusting that all that I reveal to you will only bring you closer.

Beloved,

Glad to report, I seem to be taking better care of myself these days—maybe because I'm noticing it sooner when I'm not. I'm much more aware when I settle for not quite it or less than what I really want. Do I deserve to have what I really want? Yes! And not because I am any more special or deserving than anyone else. For any one of us to have the life that we want, we have to believe that we deserve it. Otherwise we end up sabotaging the good that does come to us.

Ah, but in this moment, I feel so good. In this moment, I am eager, excited, and there is nothing that I lack. And so, in this moment, I am deeply connected to the current of life that is flowing through me and bringing me you! How sweet to feel this current . . .

I see myself sitting by a river, trailing my hand in the cool water, at peace with me and musing about you. I see you as you sit in a small boat, drifting downstream, at peace with you and musing about me. There is nothing to do but allow the current to bring us together—a current set in motion long ago. There is nothing to do but enjoy the river, the peace, and this sweet anticipation.

Dearest Beloved,

This morning grey clouds are floating westward across the wet silk of a pale sky. A Course in Miracles lies open in my lap and I read: "Only holiness will content you . . . Call forth the holiness in others . . . In holiness, nothing is hidden."

Yes, that is what I want with you. When nothing is hidden, true communion can happen, even without words. I want to stand in that Light with you where a deeper truth of what we are is revealed.

May we look into each other's eyes with total openness and willingness to see and be seen . . . looking past all thought . . . and each seeing and calling forth the holiness of the other. After all the life we've lived, I have a feeling that nothing else will content us. Nothing less will do.

Dearest Beloved,

Sometimes I still find myself searching for an image of God to worship. I remember the adoration I felt gazing at the face of my first spiritual teacher, or into the eyes of a lover, or at the perfection of my newborn child. Yet, moments of longing and adoration arise and disappear. And in all the unremarkable spaces, there is emptiness.

I breathe into this emptiness. I trust that even if I cannot see it, there is no space without Radiance. Whatever it takes for me to allow the Divine to enter and take up permanent residence in my awareness, I am willing. Whatever it takes.

Sometimes I wonder if that means giving up my desire for this relationship. Maybe. It's funny but this fantasy will end either by you showing up or by me no longer feeding it with my attention. But the desire is not just for an intimate relationship but also for the experience of Oneness, and my whole life dances in and out of this desire.

In my imagination, you burn with the same longing for Oneness, and our longing will some day be answered with the gift of each other. Time and again, experience has shown me "to ask and it is given". At this point, it's harder to believe that you won't come than it is to believe that you will. And that feels good.

And so, be patient, Self. It must be so.

I am more well with missing you than content
with all the physical wonders of this world.
~ Mirabai

Sweet Friend,

Writing in this book makes me happy. Because while I am focusing here—on you—I feel the love. And every time I focus on this relationship and feel this love, I am adding energy to this creation, this connection between us. I believe you are also flowing energy into this connection with your thoughts and desire and your own imagination.

A Course in Miracles teaches: "All thought creates form on some level." With all this focused energy and thought, this connection between us had to condense into material form at some point—and the first condensation is this book. This connection already has a life of its own—it's pulling us to it—just as this book also has a charge, an attractive force that sends out signals to those who also seek the spiritual path of relationship.

Essentially, we are love, and we yearn to express that which we are. Perhaps it's true that an opportunity to express love arises in every moment but it's just so easy to miss in our habitual state of distraction! And yet, every in-breath is a chance to take in grace. Every out-breath is a chance to give something back. Life is so simple when I remember this.

Beloved,

Today I write for the purpose of connecting to peace.

I'm right on that edge again—breezes from the other side reach me here, the wind of remembrance, and I almost wake up. I feel like I've been drugged by the thoughts of this world and I'm struggling to awaken from a colorless dream. I yearn to feel my Self again.

Sometimes when I come to this edge, I may look for someone to pull me over to the other side. Or I try to distract myself with books or work. Sometimes, thinking I can just outrun it, I put on my shoes and race down the bike path toward that sweet state of endorphinated freedom.

But I wonder what would happen if I just allowed this feeling— this strange soup of desire, grief, poignant memories, wisps of faith, spasms of impatience? What if I allowed this edgy part of me to be—with no judgment and no resistance to it? Would I disappear into it? Would it keep me from my destiny or lead me deeper into it?

When you are here, I will ask you all these questions in person and somehow, I don't think I will need an answer from you. Your being is part of the answer. I imagine your breath is part of the breeze that sails me over to the other side. Hmmm, and I can choose to remember that even now, somewhere on this planet, you are breathing. You are breathing the same earth-enveloping, body-embracing, sense-expanding air—right now—as I am.

And with this remembering, I am almost there.

Beloved,

I put pen to paper not knowing what I want to write to you. I only know my heart is so full and happy and that I hope that some of this joy will overflow into words that somehow, someday will reach you. I know that on one level they reach you at the very instant in which I offer them. That is the magic and the mystery of this connection.

There is a freedom in knowing that love is not bound by the lesser laws of time and space. This freedom comes from trust in the grace that guides the unfolding of the cosmos, and this same freedom says yes, you can play in this life according to the dictates of your heart. You are free to listen to the longings of your soul and follow them and learn from them and, best of all, enjoy them.

In this play I am following a vibrational trail to you. I notice the signs along the way that say I'm getting closer. Excited by every clue, I walk the path gratefully, gathering gifts for you along the way. Adorning myself with moments of joy, with jewels of presence and the fragrance of peace, I prepare myself for you.

To My Lover,

I want you. And I want to want you. I want every nuance of ecstatic sensation possible within the experience of this connection. I want to travel further into the wild and sacred spaces of sexuality with you than I have ever gone before. I want you to take me, thrill me, enjoy me, devastate me with kisses, and humble me with the pure beauty of you. I want to play with you—and I want you to feel that playing with me is one of the sweetest reasons God gave you breath. I want to co-invent with you a whole new geometry for the embodied play of these souls . . .

Imagine—someday, you will be here and I will inhale your presence and let it fill me. And how do we get to someday? Actually, we never do. We can only and always be here, and let someday arrive in the guise of today.

Beloved,

I thought of you as I walked through the woods today. In the cool green space of my imagination, I saw you. There you were, about ten feet away, looking at me. Just there, completely quiet, and there was no sense of strangeness, no urgency, no thought really. As if you had been standing there forever, waiting for me. And I knew exactly who you were.

In a way, this waiting is like being pregnant. I know this encounter, this miracle, is going to happen that will change my life forever. This person is coming into my world and I get to explore everything about this person and myself through this person and the whole world with this person . . . this human person . . . you.

Sometimes I wonder—what if we did not have eyes and ears to take life in, and a mind to remember and dream, and a language to share our experience—would not our world be so small? But all these are given so that we can walk into and explore and share each other's worlds.

May I always remember that every person is a portal into a whole other world . . . and it is always an honor and a privilege to be allowed to enter in.

My Dearest,

I have decided I must write to you every day, no matter what. When I write to you, I make a connection to something real inside myself—a real energy of love—or, at least, to my belief in love.

At times, I still get lost in a mental maze—one that always begins with self-doubt and the confusion of conflicting voices inside. Yet, when I can accept my feelings—with the help of a few slow, deep breaths—and remember I am doing the best I can, I become softer with myself. I remember I have eternity to figure this out (life) and forever in which to grow and learn.

The thought of you is like a gentle hand taking mine and leading me out of the maze. Your voice in my mind tells me softly that everything is okay and coaxes me out of the cocoon. Your face that I see as I emerge from the darkness reminds me, again and again, that I do believe in love.

Change is happening all over this sweet planet, faster than ever before, and we are a part of the change. My belief in Love is the strongest thing I have to hold onto at this time—and you are a part of that belief; you are an embodiment of that love. That is why I must write to you every day, no matter what.

Beloved,

Yesterday, I was talking with a young woman who is also longing for a partner. I heard myself suggesting that she try to relax into the feeling of longing. Maybe if she did not resist her own desire but felt it fully, then it could move. Maybe it would speak to her. Maybe her heart would open . . .

The patience that love requires of us takes so much practice, and part of the practice is simply the repetition of a truth. The soul doesn't need this repetition—it already knows this truth. That's why when we hear it something in us leans in and lights up. But the conditioned mind needs the repetition, so the old tracks in our brain that were laid down in moments of fear can be replaced by new neural pathways of trusting in Self and believing in Love.

Even though I'm not always sure about what to do, I believe in a path, my path, alongside a river of destiny that is always flowing into more and more realization of the Divine. Sometimes I can't find the river—I can't hear it because of all the noise I'm making as I thrash around in the undergrowth. But when I stop and become absolutely still—when I open to what's around me—then I begin to hear the song of the river again. As I follow the sound back to my path, I know that it will take me where I want to go and need to be. And where someday, Beloved, I will see your path crossing mine.

Beloved,

In the clear blue of this morning sky, two ospreys are circling right above me. One is flying in one direction, and the other in the opposite direction, and they are calling to each other in their high sweet voices. As they circle, they come so close, their wings almost touching. A dance. So lovely.

Perhaps our souls are dancing like this right now. Circling each other, I am traveling one way and you are traveling another. Maybe, at times, we come close to each other and almost meet. And then, disconnected or distracted or just not ready, we drift away from each other. At some point—I just know—that our lives will bring us to the same place at the same moment on this vast, beautiful Earth. At some unknown, compelling point we will turn around, see each other and understand. And it will be so natural . . . and feel so right.

What a mystery that I can taste the joy of that future moment right now. May you taste the joy of that moment, too, and may our wings touch soon.

Beloved,

Dream: I am on a path that wanders through a wood, and slopes gently up and around a mountain. I have been walking for hours—all night, in fact. But day is coming now. A distant bird calls out, another answers close by. The soft, slow light is revealing more and more the tangle of leaves, stones, fallen branches. As more light comes, I see more beauty; shapes and colors cause me to cry out in delight. I know these same forms were there throughout the night. But in the darkness, I could not see them ... I could only sense their presence, intuiting the companionship of sacred things.

What awaits me on the mountaintop? What will be revealed only in the full light of day? I don't know, but the not-knowing keeps pulling me forward, past uncertainty and fatigue—even past the present beauty. The attraction of the more that Life wants to give, to reveal, is always teasing me from just up ahead, from just around the next bend. Who will I be—there, then? Who will you be? What awaits us as we take each step in our becoming, as we continue on our paths with every choice we make ...

Sometimes, I don't even want to speculate. Sometimes it's enough just to say,

Okay, Universe, surprise me. I will leave my maps and plans, even my backpack, here by the side of the trail, and plunge ahead. I am willing for each moment to be the unknown gift that it is. May I be open to each moment just as it is.

Dear One,

A moment ago, I held this book in my lap, hands covering it like a blessing, and closed my eyes. A thought crossed my mind to prepare myself before opening the book—maybe to meditate or pray for a minute, or read some scripture. But then, the feeling of peace came into me just from holding this book.

What is this peace? Peace is the energy that doesn't ask for anything, but quietly vibrates in harmony with everything. I want to cultivate this energy simply because it has offered the most consistent source of happiness that I have ever known.

A Vision: In quiet, wordless harmony, we are wandering over open fields and meadows and climbing onto hilltops. Then, I am standing beside you and we see for miles, knowing that all that we see is also gazing back at us in loving recognition. In that moment, we feel the embrace of home, our home, the Earth. This vision and feeling are so familiar that I wonder, is this a scene from the past or the future ... or does it only exist in the timeless space of my imagination?

Past, present, future—three cords of time that are bound together with love and gratitude to create a rope strong enough to lift us up together. Whenever, wherever we transcend our belief in the limitations of time and separation, we enter the dimension of love, where all that exists is now . . . which is truly a place of freedom, an atmosphere of joy.

See you there . . .

Dearest,

The other day I was telling a friend how a certain lover could look into my eyes and make me feel—for a moment or two—that I was the most beautiful, wanted, sensual being on the planet. My friend said, "Can't you make yourself feel that way? Do you need someone else to do that for you?"

In a sense, of course, my friend was right. No one can "make us feel" something. How we feel is always an inside job, but someone else can provide the stimulus that triggers a response in us. I certainly liked the stimulus my lover was providing . . . but the question remains: Can I do that for myself?

A teacher once said that we could make ourselves feel loved and wanted but we don't consider ourselves worth the effort. So, it's a catch-22. We want to feel loved but don't think we're worthy of loving ourselves. How do we learn to love ourselves that much? To cherish being in our own company? To take as good care of ourselves as we would our child, best friend, lover? How do we learn to do that and not bump into all the years of programming about how wrong it is to be selfish and self-centered?

I remember the shame of being called "selfish" when I was a child. It was the worst thing to be! That shame was a great motivator for me to be good. And good meant learning the rules of what would please others and denying my own feelings and instincts. Years later I saw that we are only accused of selfishness when we're not doing what "they" want us to do. In other words, when we follow our own desires and not those of others—that's when we're being selfish. I've noticed how often two people who are well-practiced at not feeling their own desires can end up doing what neither really wants to do—in the name of compromise and selflessness. What a great breeding ground for resentment.

Maybe selfish is a good way to be.

In the end, what I really want is to see past the duality in my own mind between "me" and "you" . . . and see that when I do something good for me, it benefits you, and when I do something good for you, it blesses me.

Beloved,

I haven't wanted to write to you lately. I know it's partly because I've been sad and I didn't want to show this part of me to you. I always want to hide this cloudy, unhappy part because there's that shame again. I wish I could just accept and love her/me. And let her be. I remember when my kids were moody and how it never worked to try to change their moods or make them lighten up. Whenever I could let them be and love them anyway, they seemed to shift much faster. Later in life, when someone I was dating was moody or withdrawn I'd feel so abandoned and take it so personally. Maybe the roots of this reaction go back to childhood experiences of Dad being gone—first to the Korean war and then to Vietnam—and Mom trying to cope with all the kids, bills, loneliness, fear, etc., in his absence. We probably all felt abandoned but had no way to name it or talk about it.

I feel a softening inside just from writing about it.

I hope when you are here that I can talk about the not-so-pretty feelings without burdening you or expecting you to fix it. I hope that when you need time and space for yourself that I can graciously and lovingly allow that. And I pray that we can communicate our needs and desires, hopes and fears in an atmosphere of trust and acceptance. I know the more I can learn to do that for myself, the better I can do that for you.

Dearest Sweetheart,

There is a fog in my head—just behind my eyes—and it makes it hard to focus. I was trying and trying to get my thoughts lined up in some direction (choose one!) and it was such an effort. Finally I thought, let me just feel what is going on in my body. There's a pressure and it's even stronger when I try to ignore it or push through it. I think it's all my trying. Trying to be worthy, to feel good, to serve, to do all the things I do every day and do them really well so I can live a happy, creative, productive life. I'm just tired of trying so hard. I want to find and feel the flow . . .

I know this cloud of efforting is nothing, an illusion, but still it drains me. As I look into it, I discover a thought that makes me sad: Until I'm in a relationship of my dreams, I'm a failure. I don't think I've ever admitted that thought before. Here is a powerful ego-construct that, of course, I don't consciously believe. And yet I can see how I've based so much of my self-worth on whether or not I am in a relationship, and if that relationship is going well. Can I let go of this belief and not let go of the dream?

If I need you to make me feel like a successful human being, what kind of burden am I placing on you? I don't want to do that to you. May I find the compassion within to embrace all parts of me. May I remember that the love I extend—whether to myself or to others—heals us all.

Dearest Beloved,

I came so close to you the other day, it was as if you had just stepped out of the future and into the room and I could feel all your happiness at finding me. I could feel your delight as clearly as I've ever felt anyone loving me.

I realize that a part of me that has always felt unworthy of love is stepping forward now to be healed. And not healed because you are going to take away her pain, but healed because she is choosing to come forth out of the darkness, out of hiding, and to ask for what she wants. I'm grateful that, finally, I feel ready to let this happen.

I am loved. Just to accept that. The most healing truth, the most powerful undo-er of illusion: I am loved. There have been times when hearing those words spoken out loud to me released a flood of tears. And the release always felt so good—as if the grief and loneliness of lifetimes was being washed away with every tear . . . so that the healing energy of love itself could pour into every space within me.

Thank you for the love that you are.
Thank me for letting it in.

Sweet Friend,

It's becoming increasingly clear to me that more joy and freedom come from loving than from being loved. Even if all the love in the world were coming toward me, there is no guarantee that I would feel it! If I were to block it for any reason, it would be like water falling onto stone. It might make an impression but it would take a really, really long time.

We human beings find a million reasons—conscious and unconscious reasons—to block the love that is coming toward us. For it's always coming toward us, into us, from the whole Earth, the Universe, from all of creation. The most profound and powerful experience I have ever had convinced me that whatever Reality is—it loves us. When this happened to me several years ago, I was lying alone on my bed. I had spent the morning in intense grief, and then, for no reason I could discern, something let go inside me and in the next moment, I was being held in the most incredible love. And light. I was taken into absolute peace and then bliss. It lasted for hours . . . and I can assure you no mind-altering substances were involved!

Oh my Dear, right now my love joined with all love is flowing to you. I hope you are letting it in. I hope that in this moment you cannot find a single excuse to disallow this beautiful, powerful, life-giving energy. I hope that in this sweet, holy moment, all your doors and windows are wide open and you are breathing in this love. And then, when you are with me and breathing me, you will remember this moment, and know me. And I will feel familiar to every cell in your body.

Beloved,

A friend was visiting this past weekend and I got to really enjoy the companionship—that is, the feeling of another's presence in the house, over dinner, and just driving around doing errands together. I loved the light, easy conversation, the mutual teasing and having fun, the way we could touch each other with affection. It was just so nice to have a friend here and to decide together what to have for dinner, what movie to see ... to have someone beside me on the couch, rubbing my shoulders and hearing the story of my day. I loved the ease of it.

It's as if I'm only just now learning the simple joy of companionship. A part of me has always been very private and solitary—no matter how many people were around. Maybe because of self-judgment and the fear of exposure, I've kept so much to myself. But it's getting easier to share what goes on inside me. Partly because so much of it feels good, partly because of practice . . .

So, today I will practice the art of companionship with self. I will be a good friend to me, to God, and to whomever is around me. And I will think of you often and breathe into the ease and joy of you as friend. I will carry your presence around with me today, feeling how natural and effortless it is to be with you, and remembering that I don't have to wait until you are here for the "pleasure of your company". I can enjoy it—and you— right now.

And I do.

My Lover,

I like to imagine the rush I will feel when I pick up the phone and hear your voice. I like to think how easy it will be talk to you— and how sometimes our conversations will cause an explosion of new ideas to go off in my head and a hundred pathways of possibility to appear beneath my feet, each one beckoning me to some new perspective, some new vista of thought.

And sometimes, I remember that not a single word needs to be shared for a deep and penetrating conversation to take place between us that is too big for words. It is, in fact, the listening and reflection through which we come to really know ourselves and one another. It is the conversation and the context in which the meaning of our life together quietly unfolds.

Through these letters, I am listening in on this timeless conversation between us. I hope you are beginning to hear it too. And when you do, may you remember what we have already shared.

Beloved,

This will be my last letter to you—for a while. For you see, my sweet Friend, I am not running toward you anymore to escape myself. I have been fleeing "me" my whole life—except for cherished moments when I turned, surrendered and embraced me. And those were sometimes the hardest but always the truest and kindest moments of my life.

How can it be that we are taught—not intentionally, perhaps, but effectively—to dislike and distrust so much of what we are? Our bodies, emotions, intuitions, hopes . . . and even our deepest desires? And once we have learned how not to love or trust ourselves, we must then try—desperately, at times—to find love, meaning and salvation in the body of another. Yet even as we try to drown ourselves in the ocean of another's life, we are hating the water that does not let us breathe.

I am not running toward you anymore.

If you come to me in this life—if our souls are ready finally for that great dance, then so be it. I know I will feel more grateful than I can even imagine. If you don't come, then so be it. I am discovering, at last, that I carry a universe inside me and every day I am born again within it.

By the grace of God, I am forever coming home.

I love you now more than ever.

Part Three

Living the Vision

We can only learn to love
By loving.
~ Iris Murdock

Where there is great love,
there are always miracles.
~ Willa Cather

The Beginning in Time

The relationship had been launched. On some level, it was a reality, an *energetic* fact. And then, within days of putting the butterfly book down, I met him.

October 2001

I have just returned to Florida after visiting my sister in Virginia. It's late when I get home, and after unpacking and sorting through the mail, I step outside to water the little garden out front. By now it's about 2 am, and as I stand there, I look up and see two butterflies with wings outspread, facing each other right above my front door. Butterflies like this are rare on the beach where I live and yet there they are—two of them right there in the middle of the night.

I smile and say out loud, "You're getting warmer, Sweetheart."

So, yes, I had met him on that trip to Virginia, but curiously I did not 'recognize' him. On October 11th, Mike had come to a small seminar I gave at my sister's house. It was exactly one month after the tragedy of 9/11 and this seminar was called "Navigating the Dark Night." We sat on the floor in my sister's yoga room and talked about learning to see difficulties as opportunities to heal the wounds in our culture and bring light to our collective shadow. Mike didn't speak much. What I remember most about him was that he sat cross-legged on the floor and because he wasn't very flexible his knees were up near his ears! But he did have a wonderful smile on his face by the end of the evening.

During that visit, I'd also spent time with a couple of other men who were interesting and attractive. A spiritual teacher once said that we each have 20,000 soul mates—which makes much more sense than the idea that out of seven billion people on the planet there could be only *one*. So, when I saw the two butterflies above my door, I wondered about the guys I'd just met in Virginia. But having let go of any urgency to find 'him', I was content to let the mystery unfold in its own time and in its own way.

March 2002

For my birthday I go to Patricia for a conversation with her guides—the wise nonphysical friends who have provided much inspiration and clarity for me over the last few years. This time I make a request that I'd never made before—I ask if she could "bring in"

Jesus. For a very long time, I have believed that the consciousness of every awakened Master is still here and that we can and do connect with that consciousness in many ways. My connection to this beloved teacher had grown from a childhood devotion through a brief adolescent crush and into a deep appreciation through a twenty year journey with *A Course in Miracles*.4 But today I have a specific reason for wanting a more direct communication. I trust his invitation that when two or more are gathered in his name, he'll show up, and I also know that Patricia has that ability to be a clear voice for the nonphysical world.

Patricia is quiet for a while, eyes closed, head nodding. The room had already been full of light and now the light seems thicker and more golden. She says, "He is here . . . Ahh, it is liquid love." I take a deep breath and make my request: I want to be healed of the belief that having a partner would be a detour and a distraction from my spiritual path. Almost immediately, I feel pressure on the top of my head—as if warm hands are resting there. The heat on my head is comforting—strong— and my mind becomes very quiet. Patricia tells me that little pockets of belief are being cleared—the dogma of various religions from various lifetimes. Patricia then sees a lifetime in which, as a cloistered nun, I had been very, very happy being "married to God." For so many centuries, institutional religion has taught that this is the only way to experience divine union—it is no wonder that even in this life I had spent a year in an ashram where I took very seriously the vows of celibacy, poverty and obedience. But now, as this belief is being cleared, I understand that that way was appropriate for then but not for now. In this lifetime I want to surrender to the yoga of relationship, to experience the embodiment of Spirit in my Beloved, in my self, and in our union.

I take a deep breath and ask for a blessing on my path with a partner. And now the heat intensifies and moves to my heart. I start sobbing and shaking all over. I am incredulous and at that same time completely sure:

Jesus is giving me—us—his blessing.

Love is saying yes.

~~~~

April 2002

I had planned to go to a conference in New York when for some reason I change my mind at the last minute and decide to go to Virginia instead. I email my breathwork clients and those who'd been to my seminar that I was coming. Mike emails me back right away and says he want to see me.

Monday afternoon: Mike comes by and we sit in a small book-lined study in my sister's house. I learn that he's pursuing a PhD in mythology and that he wants to find a dissertation topic that has to do with ecstasy. As part of his research, he had spent time with a shaman in Arizona participating in a sweat lodge and a 'soul journey'. He also talks about boxing—the intimacy of it!—and, oddly enough, a fear of snakes. I flash on how snakes are a symbol of the Goddess, of kundalini and sexuality, but don't say anything. At one point, we stop talking and are simply gazing into each other's eyes.

I feel a tightening in my chest and, at the same time, a desire to get closer. For some strange reason, I really want to lay my head on his chest. I pull back from that desire and let it go. But as I stay attuned to him, two distinct responses are triggered in me. When I focus on my right side, I'm aware of feeling very "human" (flawed, fragile, fallible). On my left side, I feel what I would call goddess energy. It is powerful, clear, and detached. He breaks eye contact before I do. Just before he leaves, I ask if I can read him a passage from *A Course in Miracles*. He says yes, but seems completely unmoved by the reading.

When I watch Mike walk away from the house, I feel curious. I realize that I'm buzzing. And confused. There's no one else at home in my sister's big house, and I roam around wondering what to do with this strange energy inside me. Finally, I call a friend. I share what I'm feeling—oddly enough I don't really connect it to Mike because I'm not attracted to him in a way that's familiar to me! At one point, I say to my friend, "I'm ready for someone to commit to adoring me." (Even as I hear myself say it, I think what a narcissistic thing to say).

My friend replies, "And are YOU ready to commit to adoring someone else?"

I pause before I answer. I want to tell the truth here. Finally I do say,

"Yes. Yes, I am."

An email correspondence begins between us—mostly about books. One day I realize how intrigued I am by him and decide to go back to Virginia and see him again. I email him that idea. (Much later he told me that at first he thought the email was from another Elizabeth that he knew and when he realized it was from me he fell off his chair).

July 2002

Mike picks me up at the airport and ushers me into his home. I step into a large airy room that spans the whole front of the house, and immediately like everything about it. It is so tasteful with its pale yellow walls, the hand-stenciled border of a William Morris design, the old leather club chairs by the hearth, and—word-person that I am—I love the huge dictionary on its very own antique wooden stand. Then I see the stuffed coyote on top of a vintage armoire. "That's Bill," he says. "He was a gift." Okay. Next, he offers me champagne and strawberries and a tour of the house. Even though I am tentative about champagne in the afternoon, I like how romantic, how classy it is.

I think I am ready to be wooed.

~~~~

So the journey begins of getting to know each other in real time, and falling in love *in person*. Every relationship starts with two people encountering their idealized images of each other and thinking that *that's* what they love. Each person also wants to present his or her idealized image of self to the other. In other words, let me show you the 'me' that I want you to see. I'll reveal the *lovable* me. The relationships that really work are those in which the lovers see that who they really are is so much better than those idealized images could ever be. And messier. And more challenging. It is so powerful when my lover sees an aspect of me that I think is unattractive and he wants me anyway. In spite of, or even unbelievably, *because of.*

Early on, when we talked about who we wanted to be, Mike said he just wanted to be real. I said I wanted to be loving. In many ways, over the years, I have tried to model 'real' by being open and honest about what's going on inside me even when it wasn't pretty. And he has shown me consistently how a truly loving person shows up. Again, there are no mistakes. Except perhaps the ones that we need to make for the beauty they will eventually reveal.

*"There are three possible parts to a date,
of which at least two must be offered: entertainment, food,
and affection. It is customary to begin a series of dates with a
great deal of entertainment, a moderate amount of food, and
the merest suggestion of affection. As the amount of affection
increases, the entertainment can be reduced proportionately.
When the affection is the entertainment, we no longer call it
dating. Under no circumstances can the food be omitted."*
~ *Miss Manners' Guide
to Excruciatingly Correct Behavior*[4]

Courtship

Mike's home is a Craftsman Bungalow built in the
1920's that he'd had renovated and decorated in
the style of that era. As we walk around I notice a great
collection of books, quirky original art on the walls,
framed photographs of his children and spectacular lamps
and light fixtures. I love his unpretentious enthusiasm
about it all.

In the kitchen, all the appliances are vintage—they
do work, but because he never cooks, their charm is more
important than their functionality. On his 1948 Norge
refrigerator there are exactly seven magnets, and I realize
that each one is a different kind of 'queen.' They are a
queen bee, a drag queen, the Queen Mary ocean liner,
a Queen of Hearts from a deck of cards, a queen chess
piece, and two Queen Elizabeths, the First and Second.

I take notice because a few years before, on the annual women's retreat I lead, I'd been teasingly called *Queen,* and to my embarrassment it stuck. His refrigerator's been calling my name?

My tour guide takes me upstairs, which consists of one big room and a spacious bathroom. The first thing I see at the top of the stairs is an altar with a life-size wooden Buddha surrounded by candlesticks worthy of a cathedral. Above it, a stained glass window filters in soft afternoon light. I glance to my right and see a dressmaker's dummy wearing a vintage admiral's uniform. (Which he got from a thrift store and confesses to having actually worn to a company dinner). The admiral is standing beside an old green metal glider (just like the one on Grandmother's back porch) and white wicker chairs. On the other side of the stairs is a *queen*-sized sleigh bed with a leather headboard and a handmade quilt in dark green, beige and rose. The large bathroom has imported Italian tile and a claw-foot bathtub (of course!). I could definitely see myself there, luxuriating in a hot bath, gazing out through the wide windows at the back garden with its fishpond and dogwoods and lilacs. A large tapestry of a scene out of Arabian Nights hangs above the toilet and the bidet. (Yes, a *bidet).*

Mike's home is so beautiful . . . and yet it is also small, immensely comfortable, a little quirky and definitely not ostentatious. I wonder, *can you fall in love with someone solely on the basis of where and how they live?* Maybe.

~~~~

Later, we talk about dancing and I share my love for Contact Improvisation. This is an art form and a movement practice in which two or more people share a point of physical contact and then move spontaneously together. Often it feels like no one is leading—that the shared movement is just happening from a deep, wordless, instinctual place. There are no real set dance steps, it's all improvised and can be so much fun. The point of contact can move but the trick of it (and the joy) is how each one must really tune in to the other and be right in the moment. You also have to be tuned in and comfortable with yourself and your own body. Mike is wary but willing to try it with me.

We stand up, face each other and let the point of contact be our right forearms—less obvious than hands, safer than other body parts. The eye contact helps as we just begin to move around, exploring and being open to where the contact takes us. At one point, we fall down and he gets a good rug burn, but we are both 'appropriate' through this play and he's a perfect gentleman. Still, the sparks begin to fly . . . and I find myself *remembering* this energy.

That evening the conversation continues—with words this time. I sit at one end of his green velvet sofa and he is at the other end. We've been sharing histories and talking about relationships, intimacy, etc. I hear myself say, "I want to do it differently this time—relationships, I mean. I feel like I've rushed into things—too much, too fast. So before I get too involved again . . . I just want to be *sure*. I'm beginning to believe that every time you make love with someone, you give them a piece of your soul."

He is quiet for a moment, thoughtful. Then he says, "I hope so."

~~~~

Ancient lovers believed a kiss
would literally unite their souls, because the spirit
was said to be carried in one's breath.
~ Eve Glicksman

~~~~

The next day, we're headed out to lunch when I notice his license plate. It starts with the letters "YMV" which are followed by four numbers that are as familiar to me as the back of my hand. These four numbers are the exact date—month/day/year—of my birthday.

"Umm, how long have you had that license plate?"

"Several years. Why do you ask?"

"That's my birthday."

We're both quiet as we climb into the (what else) vintage Volvo. I wonder if the Universe is going a little overboard with the "signs." Am I that dense? Or are we both just resonating in a way that lets us see the synchronicities that are everywhere and always? Whatever the reason, I'm loving the romantic flavor of it all and decide that YMV just might mean "You're My Valentine."

The next few days together are easy and fun and interesting. He is calming to be around, extremely courteous, and quiet much of the time. And that energy, that intensity, that happens when we kiss—it keeps surprising me. *What is this, what's happening here?* As I'm getting ready to return home to Florida, Mike says he has to go to California in a month, and he wants me to go with him. We would meet in Santa Barbara where he'll be for the last class of his PhD program, then we'd fly up to San Francisco for a couple days. Again, I'm surprised. I can't say yes right away because of other things happening at home, but say I'd like to, and we'll see. I get the feeling this man is not used to being put on hold.

I am only home for a day when I receive two dozen red roses and a note that says, *"Elizabeth, thank you for the wonderful week. What is especially amazing is that this is just the beginning. love, m"*

~~~~

Thank you, thank you! I step out of the tub, and the awareness that Mike is going to be in my life now—for who knows how long—lands inside me. I feel startled! My god, I have just opened a window into a new world and I know that I'm going to climb through this window and wander around here and explore to my heart's content. Ahh, my heart's content. Maybe, in this world, my heart will finally be content.

And I am a window into a whole new world for him as well . . .

August 2002

I take a shuttle from the Santa Barbara airport to the hotel. The cab driver says if I'm not in a hurry, he'll take me the scenic way and not charge me any extra. I say sure and am treated to a tour of this little jewel of a town. Mike will be meeting me at the Best Western as soon as class is over. Then we'll go to an end-of-school party at a classmate's house. Later that evening, as I sit in this beautiful garden with all these interesting strangers who are having warm, witty conversations, I feel like I'm in a movie. But I'm having a great time and actually like not knowing anyone (I barely know Mike!) And maybe because no one here knows me, I feel this freedom to be any way I want to be. Somehow this "permission" translates into being more spontaneous . . . which feels like being more me.

Back at the hotel, I wake up in the middle of the night in a state of panic. As I try to articulate what I'm feeling, I realize it's fear of feeling so much for him *already*. I cry and he holds me until I fall back asleep. Two steps forward, one step back. I wake up in the morning, ready to move forward again—with him. We board the small commuter plane to San Francisco and in about an hour we are in his favorite city in the whole world.

The next evening, we're sitting in a little restaurant and he's talking about sports. I have no interest in sports whatsoever. Uh oh, I think, how can this work? We have NOTHING in common. I stop him. "I have to ask you something." "Yes?" "You do know, I mean, you realize, don't you, that for the last thirty years or more my life has been about spirituality, about seeking god?"

He looks at me and says, "Yes, I know. Why do you think I'm here?"

October 2002

We're waiting for our coffee in a crowded cafe in Arlington. As we stand face to face, I realize something and say it. "Mike, you know what you are?" "What?" he says.

"You're good. You're a good person." He looks disappointed, as if being good wasn't what he wanted to hear.

Late that night, I'm crawling into his bed and he says, "I love it that you're a bad girl." I recoil! I'm not THAT. How could he think such a thing . . .

How ironic. We've discovered that we have these opposite feelings about being good and being bad. He wants to disown his goodness because it's not sexy and I want to disown my badness because it's not "spiritual". What we disown goes into our shadow and is usually visible to everyone but us. We don't want to see it because of whatever judgments we have about it. Yet I am attracted to this shadow aspect of him and he's attracted to mine. Another reason we need the mirrors that others provide— for how can I know me without you? And how much easier to accept these banished parts when you not only accept them but embrace them? *Thank you.*

Mike invites me to go with him to his meditation seminar at the Washington Center for Consciousness Studies[5]. Wow. This is the most powerful meditation group I have ever experienced! It is led by Rudy and Sharon Bauer, and they are both highly skilled at leading people into *the Field*—the expanded state of consciousness in which it is possible to feel the energy, the openness, and the oneness of Being. This state of Being is around and within everything, and within us *as us*. The meditators at the center have been practicing both on their own and together for so many years and, as a result, the energy is intense . . . and blissful! I float out on that bliss, grateful to know that I have found another spiritual home.

Washington is beautiful and bustling as we walk downtown to Mike's boxing gym so he can work out. I have my journal and a book to read. The gym is on the fourth floor of an old building and we crowd into a creaky, dusty elevator with a few tough-looking guys. As we enter the gym, I am overwhelmed with the smell of sweaty men, a dankness heavy with testosterone. Immediately, alarms go off inside me. Mike introduces me to his coach and a few of the guys (who are all very nice) and then we go into our respective corners. His is in the ring, of course, and mine is back against a concrete wall and cardboard boxes. I watch for a few minutes and then realize I am pretty upset. I take out my journal and start scribbling furiously to try and make sense of my strong reaction and write myself into some semblance of calm. I keep writing, "why did he bring me here . . . how can he go from the peace of meditation and that amazing state of oneness to a place where grown men beat each other up for *sport* . . . who is this man . . . why am I here??"

Finally, his workout is over and we take the subway home. In a few words and with a long, dark silence, I communicate how upset I am.

Once we are home, we talk. He tells me he started boxing in high school and that it helped him to know that he could hold his own as a skinny kid growing up in Detroit. He says it's great exercise, and he even mentions that intimacy piece again—something about looking into another man's eyes and staying very present with him in a sort of dance. I don't really understand but I calm down. Once again, I see that when we find ourselves with someone who has a totally opposite view on a subject (especially one that's deeply important to us), we can close down and leave. Or we can try to lean in and understand. If nothing else, this opposite view showed me clearly how attached I am to the "rightness" of *my* view.

A few days later, I find myself angry again. This time I know it's totally my stuff and I should just let it go. I decide to change my practiced habit of keeping things to myself (especially when embarrassed about how petty I'm being), and tell him. I blurt out, "I'm mad at you and I know it's stupid but I am. I'm just angry and I don't know what to do with this!" We are standing face to face in his den.

"Do you want my boxing gloves?"

"Yes, dammit!"

He goes and gets them, puts them on me, and holds up a pillow for me to punch. I do—and it feels really good. I'm looking in his eyes and punching that pillow with everything I've got. Within thirty seconds, the anger is gone. The gloves come off. And within about thirty seconds, everything else comes off, too.

I get it. The intimacy of boxing.

Opening

Ghosts of other lovers
lie in bed with us—
And who are you?
*   And who are you?*

Ashamed of my fear
I would hide it
from you
til it creaks open
slowly,
an unlocked door
in the night . . .

The body has a knowing,
safe, here,
with you—
But the mind
holding history
holds back.

A child pulls a shoebox
from under the bed
and you offer secrets,
and trust,
with no strings.

And slowly, slowly,
the moon rises somewhere,
the moon rises somewhere,
spilling light
on this path

of you.

Our visits get longer and more frequent. When we're separated, we have dates over the phone. But we don't talk or email every day and at first I'm worried when several days go by with no word from him. In the past, that *meant* something, and so I get to notice my assumptions and expectations. One of his classmates from his PhD program had called him the 'mystery man' because he never spoke much in class. So, yes, sometimes his quietness challenges me. And sometimes I remember to go inside and through my connection to *myself* find my connection to him again. Inside to inside. Then I can ask him what's going on, and have it come from a place of love and curiosity instead of anxiousness. I'm also finding that every time I open up from a vulnerable place or ask him about something important to me, his responses floor me. They are deep, thoughtful, honest and kind. A 'man of few words' is okay—very okay—when those few words are the right words.

~~~~

November 2002

I'm doing some house cleaning when I come across the butterfly book. There are still some blank back pages so I decide to write him another letter.

> *Dearest Mike,*
>
> *Four months ago you made love to me for the first time. I still didn't know then that I had been writing this book for you. I'm glad I didn't know. The slow unfolding of this love story has been a gift. Finally, I was not impatient, not*

rushing to open the present or give my heart away or skip to the last page of the book before reading the beginning. I was no longer looking for the guarantee of a happy ending.

Now I am loving you. Now, everyday, I feel amazement and wonder that we have finally arrived in each other's lives. I feel amazement and wonder at how much I love every piece of you that you open to me, that you share with me. I feel amazement and wonder at how I find myself revealing parts of me that I have never shared with anyone and at how you embrace each part with so much gentleness, acceptance and love. And then—yes—I feel not just amazed but astonished and entranced that I follow you so eagerly through new landscapes of pleasure . . . and let you open me to my own sexual depths. You awaken the Goddess in me . . . who can then do the same for you . . .

You smiled at me and said, "We are going to have the most amazing love affair for the rest of our lives." And I know with the deepest gratitude that what you say is true.

Elizabeth

~~~~

Take a lover who looks at you like maybe you are magic.
~ Frida Kahlo

~~~~

It is a beautiful morning and we are sitting outside on his deck when I decide to tell him about the letters. I take his hand.

"So, umm, Mike, I want to tell you something and I know this might sound a little strange . . . but the fact is that I was writing letters to you before we met . . . of course, I didn't know it was *you* then because I didn't know you yet. But every morning for about a month, I wrote to my "beloved" in this beautiful old Japanese book. I called it the Butterfly Book because it had no words just butterflies on all the pages. And so, they became a symbol of this love. This love for you—you were the *unknown Beloved*. See, even then, you were a mystery man! Anyway, after a while whenever I would see a butterfly, I would think of you. Or I'd think of you *and then* see butterflies. These synchronicities said to me that we were attuning to each other—they felt like a sign that you were coming—and I'd just get happy. *(I pause. Is this all just a little too weird for him?)* So, yes, I was already loving you before we ever met. And I think that the letter-writing helped to bring us together."

Mike just sits there with furrowed brow, perhaps wondering how to respond to this. I know this kind of thing holds no weight with his practical, skeptical, where's-the-research-on-this mind. But then, as if on cue, a butterfly shows up and starts flying all around and in between us. He looks at the butterfly, looks at me, watches the butterfly a little more. I would love to know what's going through his head right now . . .

~~~~

We've been seeing each other for about five months. During one of these calls, I get up my courage and say,

> "I need to ask you something. I have all these strong feelings for you . . . but I want—at some point—I want a committed relationship. Not necessarily to get married again, but to be in a monogamous, committed relationship. I know that you've been single a long time, and that's worked for you. That may be the lifestyle that's best for you and, of course, there's nothing wrong with that. But before I invest any more of my heart in this relationship . . . um, I'd like to know what you're thinking about . . . in terms of 'us' . . . and the future."

Then I stop and hold my breath. It's quiet on the other end. Then I hear him say,

> "Well, I think I'd like to be with you all the time."

I let out my breath. Surprise and relief. And a deep rush of love.

Earth Made Glad

The Earth is glad when you see her.
The Earth—like every other female body—
is glad when you truly see her.

The Earth is glad when you love her
She—like every other female body—
is so glad when you love her.

And when you touch her—
in the way that a parched tongue
            touches water
in the way that the gasping hand of
            a new father touches
                    his child
in the way that your eyes touch the face
            of one who is slipping away
                    into that free night

When you touch the Earth in this way,
then She—like every other female body—
knows that you see

How beautiful is Her need
for love.

A successful marriage requires falling in love
many times, always with the same person.
~ Mignon McLaughlin

Why Marriage

January 2003

It's New Year's Eve and we are staying in a tiny cabin on a small barrier island off the coast of north Florida. The island is privately owned and to get there you have to drive through another island which is a nature preserve. There's no one around for miles and miles. It's very romantic in spite of the fact that all the running water smells like sulphur and the beautiful lights across the bay are from a power plant! Also, there is no heat, it's the coldest day of the year, and the kitchen faucets don't work so we do our dishes in the bathtub—kneeling and bending over the stinky water. Still, we're so happy to be here.

First night there, he says, "There's something I've been wanting to ask you."

"Okay, what is it?"

"Hmmm . . . not quite ready yet."

Next afternoon we are huddled under the blankets trying to stay warm (champagne and body heat are helping) and all of a sudden he sits up and with a big smile says, "I want to ask you *now*. Elizabeth, will you marry me?"

Without thought or hesitation, I say yes.

Several hours later, thought has come back and brought hesitation with it. We are sitting at the creaky dinner table, eating the warmed up lasagna I'd brought from home. Finally, I have to say to him:

"Mike, I'm not going to hold you to that proposal—you weren't completely sober when you asked … and neither was I when I said yes."

"Well, I meant it then and I still do. I want to marry you."

"Oh. I just . . . I have to admit that I'm just not sure. I want to say yes but I want my yes to be *one-hundred-percent*. And I'm not there yet."

He looks crestfallen, and a little confused. He's very quiet.

"I'm sorry. I'm not saying *no*, I just need us to talk about this more. Please say something!"

"Well, this is new to me. In the past, I was usually the one not willing to commit."

We finish eating and cleaning up in the chilly silence. The dishwater smells worse than ever, and we decide to leave the cabin early the next morning and go somewhere warm and comfortable.

The next day on the road to St. Augustine, I ask him, *"So, why marriage? Why do you want to be married? At this stage in our lives, we don't 'need' to get married. So what would marriage mean to you now?"* Thus we begin a conversation that continues off and on for the next three days. Over dinner, we compare notes on what worked and didn't work in past relationships. While walking through old neighborhoods, we talk about what commitment means to us. We play Scrabble on the huge four-poster bed and make up our own words. We define love for each other in verbal and nonverbal ways.

A couple days later, we are back at my house. It's twilight and we are just quietly holding each other. All of a sudden, I realize how loved I feel, how much in love I am, how being together is so good, so right.

I ask him to marry me. He doesn't hesitate—*Yes!*

That evening when my eighteen-year-old son comes home, Mike pulls him into the next room. "Chris, I'm in love with your mother and I want to marry her. Would you be okay with that?" A few moments later these two smiling men come into the room where I'm sitting. I am silly with happiness.

~~~~

Fast-forward ten years, I'm working on this part of the book and I text Chris:

> *"So what did you say and feel when Mike asked you about marrying me?"*

> *His first text comes back: "Hmmm I don't remember what I said exactly but I know it ended with him on the ground and me with a really sore fist."*

"Haha. That was another guy. Be serious."
I hit send.

Chris: "Okay . . . I really don't remember what I said but I remember being so happy and kind of honored to feel grown up enough to have him ask me. I also felt proud of you for having such a good man show so much respect for you and me. It was one of the happier moments I have probably ever had—come to think about it."

"Wow. Am now crying. So glad I asked! Yay love!"

"Yay love!"

Things He Said

"Sophistication is overrated."
And then, I liked him very much.

Ashamed of my poverty, I sat before him.
"You've been pursuing other goals."
And then, I loved me more.

"Yes, I hope so," he says, "that when you have sex,
you give a piece of your soul."
And then, I began to believe in him.

"We'll do whatever it takes to make it work."
And then, I knew I loved him.

I never took my children sailing round the isles of Greece,
skiing in Vermont, on holiday in Spain.
Christmas was from Wal-Mart, clothes were from consignment,
and meals were tofu, rice and beans.

"But you gave them other things."
And then, I knew

that they would love him, too.

March 2003

We've been engaged for a couple months when one night I find myself wandering around his house in Virginia, unable to sleep . . . *again*. I pull a book at random off the bookshelf and spend the whole night reading the myth of Inanna[6], the Queen of ancient Sumer who must go into the underworld in order to become her fully awakened Self. As she descends, she is stopped at seven different gates and at each one she must strip off a layer of clothing or jewelry, all of which are symbols of her identity and her power. At the lowest level of hell, she is killed and her corpse is hung up on a peg. She is eventually rescued and emerges as the Goddess she was meant to be. I am so relating to Inanna right now—the descent part, not the Goddess aspect. I realize that when I'm here at Mike's house I am not *who I think I am* in Florida. That is, I've left behind all these identities that have been my "secure" base. At home, I'm a counselor, teacher, mother, daughter, and friend. I'm a respected member of my family and community, and I've worked hard to earn and to own these identities and to be good at all these roles. Through this sleepless night, I get to see painfully how much of my self-worth is based on what I can do for others. But am I doing for others ultimately just to be able to feel good about myself? Here in Virginia, a thousand miles away, what am I? A nobody who is about to become a *wife* again—a role I've already failed at once! Something in me recognizes this as *ego death* and knows that it's an inescapable part of this evolutionary journey. Something in me hopes that, like Inanna, I will come through this more awake, authentic and empowered. But some very loud parts of me don't trust that and are simply freaking out.

The next morning over coffee, I tell Mike that I need to talk to him. I tell him that I didn't sleep at all the night before and all these fears are coming up. Then—through my tears—I say, "I don't think I can marry you!"

The brow furrows. Then he looks at me and says,

"Well, maybe instead of planning a wedding, we should be going to a counselor." And then he suggests that we go to the very counselor whose book on marriage we are reading. Relief floods through me as his calm answer just wiped out half my fear.

Shift

Four a.m. — Thoughts I can
push away in the daylight
stand round the bed like boogeymen
triggering the alarms
of childhood.

Eight a.m. — With coffee and prayer
and the calling of birds,
the same thoughts are flies,
and I swat them away
with a breath.

Time is faster now and the shift between
real waking and real sleeping
happens a thousand times a day—
Look! No more ropes to hang onto or
for hanging—

Only an inner cord tied to the invisible
that keeps getting stronger
and keeps
swinging
me up.

The New Age man and the New Age woman are not perfect, totally developed individuals. Rather, they are individuals who look for the reasons for their lack of fulfillment just as much in themselves as in the other. Thus they can recognize a negative mutuality that needs to be worked on together.

They do not assume a stance of self-righteous blame to widen the gap between self and other, between self and truth.[7]

~ *Eva Pierrakos*
Pathwork Lecture 229[8]

Challenge and Choice

When I was writing the letters to my Beloved, I knew I was choosing to believe in the power of imagination. I was less aware that I was also enlisting the transformative force of *intentionality*. By writing as freely and honestly as I could, I was sowing the seeds that would eventually bear fruit in every aspect of our life together. Through the letters, my intention of how I wanted to show up in relationship was crystallized and strengthened—so that when I was finally with Mike, the energy of that intention was there for me, helping me to stay more conscious, present and heart-connected through the inevitable ups and downs that were to come.

~~~~

Where did you go?

We'd only been together a few months when I encountered for the first time a part of Mike that would be most challenging for me. He had gone to his boxing gym one morning while I enjoyed yoga and reading on the sunny back deck of his home in Virginia. When he returned a couple of hours later, I jumped up, happy to see him. He did not return my enthusiasm, and seemed instead to be disenchanted that I was there! I was startled. I waited til he'd had a chance to get some water and sit down on the sofa in the den, then I asked him if something was wrong. "No, why?" he said. "You seem distant." "I'm fine." "Oh, okay." He didn't seem to want any further conversation so, feeling unsettled and confused, I went for a walk.

As I walked around the neighborhood, I thought about the difference between the Mike I knew with the warm, open heart and a light behind his eyes—and this Mike who seemed emotionless, blank and far away. Of course, first I wondered what I had done or said to make him shut down. But I quickly decided that if his mood was about him—and not about me—then I just wanted to let it go. And if he was really 'fine' and I was imagining or projecting something onto him that wasn't there, then I could choose to let that go, too. If it was a combination of our energies (which was most likely), I could even let that go and focus on finding my own center, my own peace. That was *my* job. So, as I walked, I took a lot of deep breaths and consciously noticed and appreciated the beauty of the neighborhood. When I got back to his house an hour later, I was okay. I was connected to me again.

It was such a gift that this happened early on in our relationship to show me that it was *possible*—that it could be just this simple to resolve the tension. It's a blessed aspect of new love that it shows us that we are capable of a great generosity of spirit. Eros in full bloom brings out our better selves. As familiarity eases us out of the romantic, walking-on-air stage of relationship (and it will), we can remember this. We can remember that we have this capacity, this innate and loving *Self-energy*, and we can do the work necessary to release what blocks it. Also, the more we can be in Self, the more we see it in others, and that in turn activates and strengthens this energy/consciousness, this *Presence* in them.

What often happens though is that as Eros wears off, we see that we're once again mixed up with an ordinary person with all kinds of flaws and his or her own unique oddities. Sometimes we think we fell in love with an image, an act or a projection, and then we may even feel betrayed or resent the person for "fooling us". What's closer to the truth is that we saw and loved their true Inner Being but when we're love-intoxicated, we don't remember that very few people actually live from and in the Self every day. I wonder—would we even be attracted to those who do live there more than we do? Or would we just put them up on a pedestal and keep our distance?

A Fraction of Faith

I notice Mike is not in the room. I scan the rows of chairs, I watch the doors. How can he not be here? We are here for *us*.

The seminar on sex and spirit goes on, but it's hard to listen. At the next break I run out of the room, down the hall, up two flights of stairs, down another hall and burst into our room. He's sitting on the bed reading a book.

"What's wrong?" I say.

He glances up. "Nothing."

"Well, why didn't you come to the session?"

"Didn't feel like it. I needed a break."

"A break?"

"Yes."

I am stumbling in my mind. This seminar means so much to me. It's about making our relationship better, deeper, more intimate. I'm becoming more and more upset by the minute. I'm making his not-wanting to participate in the seminar into his not-wanting us to be better. I haven't yet realized that he doesn't need us to be better or more connected. I haven't yet seen—or allowed myself to see—that it's my fear, my lack of trust in us and in my capacity to love, and my judgments about him that create distance between us and that make me want this kind of seminar so much. His willingness to come here tells me that he will do whatever it takes to make this relationship work. His unwillingness in this moment triggers something in me and I feel desperate.

We exchange some words—who knows what they were—but next thing I know I'm telling him to *go ahead and leave then!* And he walks over and starts packing his bag. All of a sudden I see so clearly that if he leaves it will be because I let him—I let him leave by letting my ego have the last word instead of my heart. And if he leaves that could very well be it for us. Do I want that? Don't I know enough now to see that when ego, pride, anger, or fear win, no one wins? Something shifts inside. It doesn't feel like swallowing my pride or giving in—more like having more faith in love than in my need to be separate—but just a fraction more. Just a fraction more.

"Mike, please don't go. I'm sorry, I don't want you to go . . ."

And he doesn't.

June 2002

We've just arrived in Colorado for a counseling intensive with a well-known marriage therapist, and we're sitting on an outdoor patio of a restaurant. A creek is flowing right by our table and there are lush green woods beyond the creek. Our conversation drifts to our childhood beliefs about God. Mike talks about the guy who drove the bus for vacation Bible school. He was happy and kind and loved everyone. I wonder how the bus driver would feel if he knew he was being remembered decades later as someone's first real spiritual teacher. The way Mike speaks of him is a teaching in itself and I take it in.

A few days later, it's midafternoon and we walk out of the therapist's office, feeling clearer, lighter, and more connected. We drive to a nearby mountain and as we climb I have a strong sense of having been here before—but I know I haven't. A two-hour hike takes us up a winding trail through woods, and we play with wedding ideas. The climb gets steeper near the rocky crest and I'm amazed to see bits of quartz crystal everywhere. At the very top, there's a cluster of large boulders, a natural lookout. We scramble up and, from 12,000 feet above sea level, we gaze out in all directions. After all the talking and processing of the last few days, there is no need for words here. We sit for a long time as the mountain hums and the wind sings around us.

> *A Vision: In quiet, wordless harmony, we wander over open fields and meadows and climb hilltops. Then, I am standing beside you and we see for miles, knowing that all that we see is also gazing back at us in loving recognition. In that moment, we feel the embrace of home, our home, the Earth. This vision and feeling are so familiar that I wonder, is this a scene from the past or the future . . . or does it only exist in the timeless space of my imagination?*
>
> *~The Letters*

We're starting to leave when I see a slip of paper stuck between some rocks. I pull it out, a pencil drops out too, and I realize that it's there for people to write about their experience on this mountaintop. We sit back down and I start to read some out loud. As I read one from a woman who is mourning her brother, Mike breaks down. He lost his only sibling some years before and something about this moment—and maybe the four days of therapy—allows a huge release of grief and guilt and love.

A few moments later, huddled together again in an even deeper state of oneness, of peace, we open our eyes. Sitting on a rock about two feet away is a butterfly. She's facing us, not moving. And now, my logical, skeptical fiancé jumps up and says, "It's a sign! We're supposed to get married right here!"

I have to laugh. There's no way our parents and friends and family would be able to make it all the way to Colorado—much less to the top of the mountain! But not wanting to rain on this incredible moment, I stand up, take his beautiful hands in mine, and say, "I, Elizabeth, take you, Mike, to be my husband and partner forever and ever. I do, I do, I do!

Miracles occur naturally as expressions of love.
The real miracle is the love that inspires them. In this
sense everything that comes from love is a miracle.
~ A Course in Miracles

October 2003

On the two-year anniversary of the day we met, our wedding takes place at twilight on a deck overlooking the ocean. There's classical Indian dance and live music, and two readings. My niece (who first suggested to Mike that he should meet me) reads a poem by my talented brother Pete, and a friend does a hilarious Southern Belle rendition of a David Whyte poem! Our two officiants make an unlikely pair. My longtime friend Rose is a petite Unity minister and Bishop King is a very tall African American priest at the Coltrane Church in San Francisco. Rose wears a simple pale blue dress, and Bishop King has on the full regalia of an archbishop in the African Orthodox Church. Our seven children and one son-in-law are our wedding party and I walk down the aisle to a song my son wrote. The hotel pool is nearby and I love seeing the three wide-eyed little girls in wet swimsuits creep up and watch our wedding. The ceremony ends with Bishop King's wife Mother Marina singing Coltrane's "Love Supreme" while the Bishop plays the saxophone. Later, the full moon rises over the waters as we dance and celebrate with family and friends. Our kids bond with each other over shots at the bar and then make hilarious toasts to us. On top of the cake are, of course, two beautiful and delicious butterflies.

And once again, a new chapter has begun.

Said Rabbi Akiva, 'If a man and a woman are worthy,
the Divine Presence rests between them.'
~ Talmud

Ever After

As I wrote in the very first paragraph of this book our
'happily ever after' has not always been easy. There
were many rough times in the first few years together
when I wondered if we would make it. I have long believed
that most (if not all) relationships progress from the
honeymoon stage into the working-through stage (where
our ego-stuff hits the fan), and then and *only if they work
at it*, will a couple move into a stage of experiencing true
love. Where there is true love, then the relationship still
includes *Eros* (romance), sexual attraction and enjoyment,
but through ongoing sharing, through deep and honest
revealing of self to other, there is also friendship, mature
love and appreciation. I believe we made it through the
tough times because of mutual respect, the commitment
we'd made, and the use of counseling whenever we
couldn't talk through by ourselves what was coming up
for us. Yes, we loved each other but love without trust is
not enough. We had enough trust in ourselves to explore
trusting each other. So instead of every hurtle and hard

time pulling us apart, they brought us closer and even more *in-trust* with each other.

You may remember that I encountered the first butterfly in the Sedona canyon and that she led me to a clearing where I received a healing, a release from the past. And then, two years later, I was astonished to learn that Mike had been hiking in that same canyon on that same sweltering afternoon. Sometimes I wonder if, as I was lying on the stone in the clearing, he was passing by just a few feet away on the path. I wonder if even then that sudden wind was merging my essence with his.

You never know! What a potent truth that is. Remembering that we don't know can ease us into the state of mind that loves the mystery and *allows* for the miracles. When we find ourselves worrying about what we don't and can't know, we can choose to let go and trust. Yes, trust is a choice, and faith is found and can only grow through practicing that choice. There is something about our ability to trust and our original innocence that brings to mind Jesus' words about the children—that "of such is the kingdom of heaven". When we drop the mind that thinks it knows and become more child-like (yet not childish), we enter the kingdom of heaven—which is none other than this free and present moment. And this free and present moment is where we have to *be* in order for love to happen.

So, do I really know that writing those letters brought my Sweetheart into my life? No, but I do know that the process helped me become more honest with myself, and more relaxed and patient on the whole subject of relationship. And the more I wrote, the happier I felt and the more I trusted love. But are we together because of the letters and the law of attraction? Or because of destiny, karma or pure chance? Magic, law or luck? Maybe all of it factors into what brings people together. Mike has always believed he's lucky (what a great belief to have!), and I have made a practice of believing in love. We know that together we are lucky in love indeed.

~~~~

The sky is clear, the sun is bright, and I am walking on the path. I feel no heaviness, only contentment and appreciation for the beauty that I see all around me . . . and for the peace that I feel inside me.

All of a sudden the butterfly appears on the path ahead. She does her sprightly air dance towards me as I stand completely still. I love watching her. She flies right up to my heart and then away again and down the path. She flutters off into the woods and once again I follow. After a few moments, I find myself in the clearing. But this time I am not alone—the Beloved is sitting on the large flat stone in the center. He looks up at me, reaches for my hand and I join him. We rest quietly on the smooth, solid altar of our relationship, and we are glad to have this time together. For from time to time we wander away from the clearing and for a few days or weeks (or lifetimes?), we go our 'separate ways.' And then, from these journeys we bring back gifts to each other—gifts that provide a counterpoint and an enriching and sometimes challenging complexity to our oneness. We would have it no other way.

But we always return to Here . . . we know this place. It is a place beyond space and time—a clearing in the heart where our souls first sensed each other and a home to which we return with deep appreciation. It nourishes us, and our hope is that through us it nourishes others as well.

Notes

1   Simon Garfield, *To the Letter: A Celebration of the Lost Art of Letter Writing.* New York: Gotham Books, 2013.

2   Kanzaka Zekka, *A Flight of Butterflies.* (New York: The Metropolitan Museum of Art and Thames and Hudson, 1979)

3   *A Course in Miracles.* Tiburon, CA: Foundation for Inner Peace, 1975.

4   Judith Martin, *Miss Manners' Guide to Excruciatingly Correct Behavior.* (New York: W.W. Norton & Company, 2005)

5   Dr. Rudy Bauer, a Gestalt psychologist, and his wife, Sharon Bauer, a skilled psychotherapist, established the Washington Center for Consciousness Studies whose purpose is "to enhance the study and practice . . . of becoming aware of the nature of awareness itself." *www.MeditateLive.com*.

6   Diane Wolkstein and Samuel Noah Kramer, *Inanna: Queen of Heaven and Earth.* (New York: Harper & Row, 1983). Mike's many books on mythology have been a source for me of "support for meditation upon one's relationship with self, others, nature, and the sacred." See also *Pagan Meditations* by Ginette Paris. (Connecticut: Spring Publications, 1986)

7   My husband is less than comfortable being called a 'New Age Man'. So let's just say he's not.

8   Eva Pierrakos, from *The Pathwork Lectures.* These lectures given by Pierrakos have been invaluable in my own understanding of Spirit, healing, purpose, love and wisdom.

A wonderful book of her essential teaching is *The Pathwork of Self-Transformation* (New York: Bantam Books, 1990). The lectures are available in entirety and for free at this website: www.Pathwork.org.

About the Author

Elizabeth Hess Stamper, M.S., is a psychotherapist, retreat leader and Interfaith Minister. A passion for exploring consciousness, meaning, the relief of suffering (personal and global), and the embodiment of joy has led her on a path of personal growth and spiritual practice since 1972. With extensive training in transformative breathwork, energy healing, Internal Family Systems, and meditation, she brings a holistic and experiential approach to helping people live happier, healthier lives.

Other work includes:
Believing in Love: Sexuality and Healing in Spiritual Relationship (available in paperback and e-book)
Two meditation CD's: *Meditations for Morning and Evening* and *Sea of Light*

For more information on writing workshops and retreats, and audio lectures on spiritual growth, visit:

www.ElizabethStamper.com

About the Author

Printed in the United States
By Bookmasters